The Dawn

ADRIAN M. HURTADO

ISBN: 978-1-969865-19-0 (sc)
ISBN: 978-1-969865-20-6 (e)

Rev. date: 010/06/2025

Dedicated to my Lord and Savior
For blessing me with a lifetime of dawn

The night is drawing near its end
The dark will soon be gone
Now comes the time I love the most
The early light of dawn

I rise from bed and draw the blinds
And marvel at the sight
Of the beauty that does touch my life
At dawn's first early light

The rising sun is picturesque
The earth looks fresh and new
Washed by Mother Nature's hand
With gentle drops of dew

I don my clothes and step outside
Into the morning air
What wonder and enjoyment
Surround me everywhere

I'm captured by a gentle breeze
That cools the early morn
A breath of life, as if the earth
Was recently reborn

Flowers open to the light
Resemblance of a yawn
They need no clock to wake them up
They recognize the dawn

I gaze at mountains far away
So mighty and so bold
The snow that rests upon their peaks
Adds just a touch of cold

The wind has caused a tree nearby
To hang its branched low
One brushes up against my arm
As if to say hello

The beauty that envelopes me
With each morning light
Astounds me to think all of this
Was hidden by the night

But time must pass, before too long
The dawn I love will leave
And when it's gone I know that its
Departure I'll not grieve

For though I long for it to stay
I feel or show no sorrow
Because I know that there will be
Another dawn tomorrow